Images of Modern America

California's Capitol Corridor

This map shows the 17 Amtrak stations on the 170-mile Capitol Corridor in Northern California. (Courtesy Amtrak.)

FRONT COVER: A special Amtrak train breaking an inauguration banner at the Southern Pacific depot in San Jose, California (Photograph by author; see page 10)

UPPER BACK COVER: Ex–Santa Fe GE DASH 8-40CW 803 leading a westbound BNSF container train at Hercules (Photograph by author; see page 60)

LOWER BACK COVER (FROM LEFT TO RIGHT): A visiting Swedish Railways ABB X2000 train (Photograph by author; see page 44), an anniversary train ride for Altamont Commuter Express (Photograph by Jon Pullman Porter; see page 38), former Canadian National Railway FP9A 6304 (Photograph by author; see page 65)

Images of Modern America

California's Capitol Corridor

Matthew Gerald Vurek

Arcadia Publishing

ISBN 978-1-4671-2417-1

Published by Arcadia Publishing
Charleston, South Carolina

Printed in the United States of America

Library of Congress Control Number: 2016940470

For all general information, please contact Arcadia Publishing:
Telephone 843-853-2070
Fax 843-853-0044
E-mail sales@arcadiapublishing.com
For customer service and orders:
Toll-Free 1-888-313-2665

Visit us on the Internet at www.arcadiapublishing.com

Dedicated to the people who operate, maintain, manage, regulate, and patronize California's Capitol Corridor

Contents

ACKNOWLEDGMENTS

The author gratefully acknowledges the assistance of the Honorable Rod Diridon Sr., Bruce Heard, Bruce Shelton, Phil Gosney, David C. Warner, Jon Pullman Porter, Gary Perazzo, Jamie Miller, John Black, and Henry E. Bender Jr. in the preparation of this book. The author also thanks the members of the Central Coast Chapter of the National Railway Historical Society and the Feather River Rail Society for their support and trackside companionship over the past quarter century. Finally, the author thanks his parents, Gerald and Ruth Vurek, and his fiancée, Peggy Haynes, for their love and support of his creative endeavors. All photographs were taken on 35-millimeter color transparencies by the author unless otherwise credited.

Introduction

December 12, 2016, will mark the 25th anniversary of Amtrak's passenger service on the Capitol Corridor, the route between Sacramento, the capital of the state of California, and San Jose, the state's first capital from its admission to the Union in 1850 until 1851. The corridor extends further east to Auburn in the foothills of the Sierra Nevada. The trackage hosts not only the Amtrak passenger trains but also freight trains of the Union Pacific (and before September 11, 1996, its predecessor Southern Pacific). Small portions of the Capitol Corridor are utilized by BNSF Railway freight trains and the passenger trains of Altamont Corridor Express and Caltrain. Light-rail systems in Sacramento and San Jose connect directly with the Capitol Corridor. In Richmond and Oakland, the San Francisco Bay Area Rapid Transit District trains stop adjacent to the Amtrak stations. The route traverses a veritable buffet of landscapes—urban-renewed San Jose, the Don Edwards National Wildlife Refuge, Bay Area suburban backyards, the industrial detritus of Oakland spiced with its redeveloped downtown, the San Pablo Bay shoreline, and the rural enclaves outside Sacramento. During the corridor's first 25 years, the railroad changed owners, new equipment appeared, Amtrak passenger service expanded from three round-trips per day to 16, new train stations were built, light-rail service expanded, another commuter train service began, and an assortment of special trains operated over the route. This book documents the Capitol Corridor, from the Silicon Valley to the Sacramento Valley, as it evolved over this time period.

The name "Capitol Corridor" was birthed from the ballot box on June 5, 1990, when California voters approved Proposition 116, the Clean Air and Transportation Improvement Act. Although a statewide act, its funding language spells out the name "Capitol Corridor" as the intercity rail service route from Placer County to Santa Clara County that received $85 million in bond money, of which not more than $35 million was allocated for railroad rehabilitation and other improvements to provide intercity rail service between Auburn and Davis.

Prior to the Capitol's startup, the only Amtrak passenger service between San Jose and Sacramento was aboard the Seattle–Los Angeles Coast Starlight (since April 26, 1982); from October 25, 1981, to September 30, 1983, the state-supported Sacramento–Los Angeles Spirit of California also traversed this route. One could also travel between Oakland and Sacramento aboard the Chicago-bound California Zephyr. The last remnant of Southern Pacific's Oakland-Sacramento local passenger service ended on May 31, 1962, when the Senator (trains 223/224) was discontinued. Oakland–San Jose connections for the overnight Lark and Daylight passenger trains were discontinued on May 1, 1960, although those trains did not make any station stops between those two cities.

The route was originally built over 100 years earlier by several predecessors of the 20th-century Southern Pacific Company (many were shell companies with equipment provided by Southern Pacific or partner Central Pacific). These predecessors include:

- San Jose & Santa Clara: 1864 by the San Francisco and San Jose Railroad
- Newark & Santa Clara: 1877 by the South Pacific Coast Railroad (leased to Southern Pacific in 1887 and subsequently merged)
- Newark & Niles (Fremont since 1956): 1909 by the Central California Railway
- Niles & Oakland: 1869 by the San Francisco Bay Railroad
- Oakland and Martinez: 1878 by the Northern Railway Company. (Note that trains were carried aboard ferryboats from Port Costa to Benicia from 1879 until the Suisun Bay railroad drawbridge was opened between Martinez and Benicia in 1930.)
- Benicia & Suisun City: 1879 by the Northern Railway
- Suisun City & Sacramento: 1868 by the California Pacific Rail Road
- Sacramento & Auburn: 1865 by the Central Pacific

Southern Pacific itself was merged into the Union Pacific Railroad on September 11, 1996, eighty-three years after the US Supreme Court ordered Union Pacific to sell its ownership in Southern Pacific, which it had controlled since 1901.

Union Pacific continues to operate freight service over the Capitol Corridor, and competitor BNSF Railway has trackage rights over portions of it as a condition of the Southern Pacific takeover. Newcomer Altamont Corridor Express (originally named Altamont Commuter Express until 2013) began operation on October 19, 1998, and provides weekday commuter trains from Stockton utilizing the route from Fremont to San Jose.

One

San Jose to Alviso

This geographical tour of the Capitol Corridor begins in San Jose, the self-proclaimed "Capital of Silicon Valley," which was also California's state capital from 1850 to 1851. It is the third-largest city in California. Until the industrial contraction of the 1980s, San Jose was a busy junction for the Southern Pacific for its routes between San Francisco, Oakland, and Los Angeles. The railroad once had two large freight-train yards along with a roundhouse to service locomotives. Operations and maintenance of the Peninsula Corridor Joint Powers Board (Caltrain) San Francisco–Gilroy commuter trains are based here. It is also the outbound terminal for Altamont Corridor Express (ACE) trains on weekdays. Amtrak's Los Angeles–Seattle Coast Starlight passenger train also makes a daily stop at the former Southern Pacific depot shared with Caltrain, ACE, and the Amtrak Capitol Corridor trains. Between October 1992 and December 1994, the former Southern Pacific passenger depot, originally opened in 1935, underwent a multimillion-dollar restoration that strengthened the depot for earthquake resistance and restored the building as close as possible to its original appearance. Santa Clara Valley Transportation Authority began service to its light-rail stop here on July 29, 2005.

Two Amtrak stops in Santa Clara were later added to this portion of the Capitol Corridor. Great America Station was opened on May 21, 1993. It was constructed under the Tasman Avenue overpass east of the station's namesake amusement park and is also an ACE stop. On July 17, 2014, the San Francisco 49ers opened their 66,500-seat football stadium just west of the station. The preserved Southern Pacific Santa Clara depot, originally built in 1864, became an Amtrak stop on May 21, 2012, after completion of an extensive platform expansion project. ACE train service also returned to this station the same month after previously stopping here from March 5, 2001, through July 29, 2005.

On the morning of December 11, 1991, Amtrak ran a special train to inaugurate its new train service on the Capitol Corridor between San Jose and Sacramento. A brand-new General Electric P32-8BWH diesel locomotive, funded by the State of California, breaks a ceremonial banner as it leads the special train at the Southern Pacific (SP) depot in San Jose.

On the back of the inaugural train was Amtrak's business car 10001, the *Beech Grove*. Its rear platform made the perfect stage for Amtrak Western Region public relations director Arthur W. Lloyd to address the crowd from at the depot on this historic day. Lloyd was one of Amtrak's first employees when it took over operation of most of the nation's remaining long-distance passenger trains in 1971.

The east side of the San Jose depot is seen here, complete with its painted-over waiting room windows and large asphalt entrance area, on October 28, 1992, shortly before the depot underwent a two-year restoration project. The Italian Renaissance Revival–style building opened in 1935 and is similar in appearance to SP's depots in Sacramento (opened in 1926) and Stockton (opened in 1930).

On April 1, 1995, the rebuilt depot now resembles its original appearance. During the restoration process, each terra-cotta roof tile was removed, stored, and reinstalled once the roof was resheathed and seismically upgraded. It was dedicated on December 8, 1994, in honor of Rod Diridon Sr., a Vietnam veteran and member of the Santa Clara County Board of Supervisors from 1975 to 1995. He also worked briefly for Southern Pacific.

With its ugly paint removed, sunlight now shines into the newly renovated interior, including the ticket counter and waiting area, as seen on October 22, 1994. The coffered ceiling's decoratively painted beams are actually made of plastic but are given a wood-like finish. Above the ticket counter is a mural by John MacQuarrie (1871–1944) that depicts San Jose as it appeared in 1935, Lick Observatory, and a train in the background clouds.

Southern Pacific control operator Don Douglas contemplates the approaching computerization of his craft inside the San Jose depot telegrapher's office on March 20, 1992. The new equipment will eventually be moved to leased office space two blocks away at 510 West San Fernando Street. Don would retire five years later after a 42-year railroad career that began with a telegraph key and ended with a computer console.

On September 18, 1992, Amtrak and Union Pacific were two of the sponsors for "Beat the Back Up Day" to promote the benefits of rail transit. In an unlikely scene for San Jose, a Metrolink passenger train (visiting from Southern California) led by F59PH 854 is flanked by Caltrain F40PH-2 904 and Union Pacific DASH 8-40CW 9455, the latter leading a train of six streamlined Union Pacific business cars.

On February 7, 2016, the National Football League's Super Bowl 50 was played in Santa Clara. Amtrak ran two additional Capitol Corridor trains to carry fans to Great America Station, adjacent to the stadium. Altamont Corridor Express ran one special train, while Caltrain ran four extra trains. BNSF Railway operated a special train composed of 12 streamlined stainless steel passenger cars led by brand-new General Electric ET44C4 3951.

When Stanford University in Palo Alto hosted World Cup soccer matches in June 1994, Caltrain borrowed several vintage passenger cars from the Golden Gate Railroad Museum in San Francisco to add capacity for the expected crowds. On June 26, 1994, Caltrain F40PH 909 is at the San Jose depot with several former Southern Pacific passenger cars; the first two ran regularly on the Caltrain route from the 1920s until 1985.

Southern Pacific's West Colton–to–Klamath Falls, Oregon, manifest freight train (symbol WCKFM) creeps slowly through the San Jose depot led by Cotton Belt GP60 9689, SD45T-2 9303, and SD45R 7431, while southbound Amtrak No. 11, the Coast Starlight, is stopped at the platform on August 12, 1995. The new Caltrain maintenance shed peeks above the Amtrak train.

In June 1995, Caltrain erected a maintenance shed for servicing its locomotives and passenger cars west of the platforms at San Jose depot, as shown on March 16, 2002. Inadequate and outdated, it was finally abandoned in 2007, when the new Centralized Equipment, Maintenance, and Operations Facility (CEMOF) opened on the land formerly occupied by the Southern Pacific roundhouse on Lenzen Avenue.

At the new platforms in San Jose, Caltrain 432, with F40PH-2 911, awaits departure to San Francisco while Amtrak P42DC 96 has recently arrived with Capitol train 729 on April 4, 2015. The Caltrain maintenance shed here was removed in 2008 and two additional passenger train platforms serving four tracks were constructed in its place. The new tracks were dedicated on February 29, 2012.

On July 11, 1993, the ABB X2000 train (built in Sweden) is towed past the San Carlos Street overpass south of the San Jose depot after a quick round-trip to Salinas as part of its demonstration run around the United States that year. With Amtrak EMD F40PH 376 and 281 providing the horsepower, the "unplugged" high-speed electric train's pantographs are stowed within its roof.

Two unique Amtrak F69PHAC locomotives, 450 and 451, were specially painted for the German Inter City Express (ICE) train's US tour and, on August 27, 1993, lead it south through San Jose. Siemens' ICE later ran in regular Amtrak service on the electrified Northeast Corridor for two and one half months beginning on October 5, 1993. The X2000 had also run on the same electrified route earlier in the year.

On April 5, 1992, Caltrain and Amtrak F40PH locomotives power Capitol No. 723 with six Amtrak Horizon fleet cars and six Caltrain bi-level coaches in tow. The train was so long that it had to venture a hundred feet or so onto the normally freight-only Southern Pacific Vasona Branch to enable it to cross over and back to the wye track to turn around for its trip back to Sacramento.

On October 1, 2005, the Santa Clara Valley Transportation Authority opened its five-mile Vasona Light Rail Extension from downtown San Jose to Campbell. Much of the route parallels the Vasona Branch, which still sees freight service. On opening day, Kinki-Sharyo light-rail vehicles 998 and 999 begin their trip to Campbell alongside the freight tracks still used by Union Pacific.

In a scene where both building and train equipment are now gone, northbound Amtrak Capitol train 726, led by EMD F40PH 369, passes the now-dismantled Southern Pacific roundhouse at Lenzen Avenue in San Jose on August 2, 1992. The roundhouse was originally built by the South Pacific Coast Railroad in 1893. Unused since July 1, 1992, it was taken apart in 2000 and stored pending its reincarnation at a new railroad museum.

In 2007, Caltrain opened its new maintenance facility at the old roundhouse site, complete with a large anvil saved from the structure's ancient predecessor. It centralized maintenance at one location and eliminated the need to send rail equipment to outside contractors for repair. Caltrain's fleet of 32 diesel locomotives and over 130 passenger cars are serviced here. This photograph shows the east side of the building on March 13, 2014.

The Golden Gate Railroad Museum's former Southern Pacific Baldwin P8 4-6-2 Pacific 2472, along with Caltrain F40PH-2 906, leads the Caltrain "Santa Train" as it approaches the junction with the Milpitas line in San Jose on December 17, 1994. The 2472 had languished on display at the San Mateo Fairgrounds since 1959, but the classic steam locomotive was restored to operating condition in 1991 after 15 years of hard work by museum volunteers.

To help promote the Operation Lifesaver railroad safety campaign to the public, Union Pacific brought its elegant E9 passenger diesel locomotives and its train of classic streamlined passenger cars to San Jose on May 17, 1997. E9A 949 and E9B 963B back their train from the College Park wye towards the San Jose depot through the area that 10 years later became the CEMOF.

Southern Pacific SW1500 2686 gently hauls privately owned business-observation car *Virginia City* past the College Park interlocking tower in San Jose on November 7, 1993. Both the tower and the car (the latter once owned by author Lucius Beebe and his partner Charles Clegg) are relics of railroading's glorious past. The passenger car is still available for charter, but the tower was closed on April 18, 1993, after being open since 1927.

The tower was still staffed on September 18, 1992, when Metrolink EMD F59PH 854 and four cars passed by en route to display at the San Jose depot. Ironically, Metrolink passenger cars would return to this trackage when Caltrain took delivery of 16 surplus cars from the Southern California commuter train service on April 3, 2015.

Weeks-old Southern Pacific AC4400CW locomotives 184 and 240 use their combined 8,800 horsepower to easily haul a train (symbol LBUTC) of empty hopper cars from the coal export pier in Long Beach past the College Park tower en route back to Utah on July 29, 1995. The station received its name from the presence of the College of the Pacific, which was located here from 1870 until it moved to Stockton in 1924.

The charred remains of the College Park tower provide a ghastly greeting to Union Pacific's Hollister Local freight train as it returns to San Jose from a voyage on its namesake branch line on June 19, 1997. The upper story was damaged in a fire of suspicious origin on March 31, 1996. About three years later, the building was finally put out of its misery and removed.

Southern Pacific's City of Industry–to–Oakland container train (symbol CIBAT), led by GP40M-2 7113, SD45T-2R 6836, and Cotton Belt DASH 8-40B 8085, marches through College Park towards the Hedding Street overpass on June 27, 1993. The concrete facility on the left has watched over the tracks since the 1940s.

In 2002, Caltrain had new equipment on order from Bombardier, but before it was placed in service, older equipment formerly used by other railroads was leased. On March 30, 2002, F40PH-2 905 leads train 175 with a Budd coach (acquired from Virginia Railway Express) and four Pullman-Standard bi-level coaches that began their careers many years earlier hauling Chicago commuters. Caltrain locomotives are usually on the opposite end of their trains.

On March 30, 2002, former Southern Pacific Baldwin 4-6-2 P8 Pacific 2472 leads the Spring Steam Special from San Jose to San Francisco with two former Southern Pacific baggage cars and many Budd single-level coaches (plus one Nippon-Sharyo bi-level coach) borrowed from Caltrain. The 2472 spent the last years of its railroad career in the 1950s hauling commuter trains between San Jose and San Francisco on this very track.

After a day on display in San Francisco, the Siemens Inter City Express train from Germany continues its California tour southbound, passing under the Hedding Street overpass on August 27, 1993. The ICE train's pantograph will not be needed during its California tour (it is being hauled by two Amtrak diesel locomotives), but over 20 years later, Caltrain's electrification project will bring overhead wires to these tracks.

Southern Pacific's eastbound Portland, Oregon–to–Los Angeles intermodal trailer train (symbol PTLAT) does not have any of its namesake railroad's locomotives as it approaches the Hedding Street overpass led by Denver & Rio Grande Western SD40T-2 5390, Santa Fe C30-7 8015, and Burlington Northern SD40-2s 7808 and 7100 on September 26, 1993. Santa Fe and Burlington Northern would announce their plans to merge as BNSF the next year.

On January 24, 1998, Southern Pacific GP40-2M 7109 shoves freight cars into Union Pacific's Newhall Street Yard after passing under the Hedding Street overpass. The yard opened in 1927 and expanded in the 1950s, but freight traffic declined precipitously in the 1980s. In 2005, Union Pacific closed the yard as a terminal and moved remaining operations to its former Western Pacific yard in Milpitas.

This January 12, 1992, photograph shows the Newhall Street end of the Southern Pacific freight yard in San Jose. SD9E 4438, still painted for the railroad's denied merger with Santa Fe in 1986, will lead that day's Permanente Local freight train. In early August 1991, Southern Pacific moved its locomotive terminal here from the crumbling Lenzen Avenue roundhouse.

The west side of Southern Pacific's freight terminal building at 795 Newhall Street is pictured on December 26, 1992. It was built in 1966 and razed in December 2007. In 2004, Union Pacific sold the land to the Santa Clara Valley Transportation Authority for use as a storage yard for the long-awaited extension of the Bay Area Rapid Transit (BART) train service from Fremont to San Jose.

Built in 1864, the former Southern Pacific depot in Santa Clara is now the oldest active railroad passenger station in California. On October 30, 2005, southbound Amtrak Capitol train 733, led by F59PHI 2010, roars past the building, preserved since 1985 thanks to the hard work of the volunteers from the South Bay Historical Railroad Society. A new train platform would open in 2012 out of view to the right.

Northbound Caltrain 437, pushed by F40PH-2C 920, is passed by Southbound Amtrak Capitol train 737 led by P32-8BWH 2051 on February 25, 2012. After nearly two years of construction, Caltrain opened its newly constructed 700-foot platform and pedestrian access tunnel at the existing depot in Santa Clara on December 19, 2011. The new platform was built in a portion of the former Southern Pacific freight train yard.

GP40-2M 7134 and GP38-2s 4802, 4840, and 4812, the locomotives for Southern Pacific's Salinas-to-Roseville manifest freight train (symbol SYRVM), move through Newhall Yard on October 1, 1995. Union Pacific closed the yard in 2005; only two storage tracks and a controlled siding are left of the once-33-track yard, now collateral damage from the changing corporate and economic landscape.

During the Union Pacific era, the scant freight train activity in Santa Clara occurs mostly at night. On February 21, 2014, signal lights cast a crimson glow over the northbound train LRQ-83, the Salinas Hauler, as it awaits a green signal to proceed north from the passenger platforms to its next stop in Newark led by GP40-2s 1447 and 1486. The light streaks are airplanes approaching San Jose International Airport.

Former Southern Pacific 4-8-4 *Daylight* 4449 is in town on July 20, 1992, as one of three steam locomotives that will star at the National Railway Historical Society's annual convention, hosted by its Central Coast Chapter. The locomotive was built by Lima in 1941 and was restored in 1975 to haul the American Freedom Train. The Santa Clara interlocking tower opened in 1927 and closed on July 17, 1993.

The Santa Clara interlocking tower is closed and awaiting preservation as Southern Pacific AC4400CW locomotives 190, 122, and 242 power another LBUTC (along with two boxcars the crew was later told by the train dispatcher were supposed to be dropped off here) on October 1, 1995. Volunteers from the South Bay Historical Railroad Society restored the tower and dedicated it as a museum exhibit on October 12, 2002.

Southern Pacific lent a locomotive clad in the railroad's final paint scheme to help speed up Amtrak train 11, the Coast Starlight, which was already three hours late on its way south to Los Angeles on March 12, 1994, led by SD40T-2 8527 and P32-8BWHs 508 and 504. The Food Machinery Corporation factory behind the train would be razed in 1998 and replaced with a FedEx terminal.

Southern Pacific's Oakland–to–San Jose manifest freight train approaches Santa Clara tower led by GP9E 3837, SD9E 4364, and GP9E 3392 on June 26, 1994. Conductor Frank Bundt rides aboard the lead locomotive's front platform. A rebuilding program in the 1970s kept many of these locomotives, originally built in the 1950s, working into the 1990s. In 2000, the Santa Clara Police Department built its new headquarters behind the tower.

Amtrak issued another visa for a foreign visitor when the Adtranz IC3 Flexliner from Denmark toured the country in 1996. On August 5, the self-propelled diesel multiple-unit passenger train passes the Agnew depot after a visit to San Jose. The depot was built in 1878 by the narrow-gauge South Pacific Coast Railroad and is now preserved by a model railroad club. The train never found any American buyers.

The new F59PHI locomotive from the General Motors Locomotive Group made its first run on an Amtrak Capitol train on September 25, 1994. It has just departed San Jose leading train 726 and will make the first stop of its trip here at Great America Station in Santa Clara. P32-8BWH 502, built by competitor General Electric, is along for the ride in case of any problems.

After Amtrak took over passenger service on several Southern Pacific routes, the railroad continued to maintain a small fleet of passenger cars for special trips. One such trip was this passenger special, led by GP60 9742 with business car *Oregon* on the rear, which ran through Alviso on October 23, 1992, in support of State Proposition 156, the (unsuccessful) Passenger Rail and Clean Air Bond Act of 1992.

On April 27, 1997, Union Pacific's Oakland–to–Los Angeles intermodal freight train (symbol IOALA), led by Southern Pacific AC4400CW 111 and SD70M 9821, is just beginning its journey south as it crosses the trestle over Guadalupe Slough. A derelict boat nestled amongst the vegetation belies the fact that Alviso was a thriving port until the late 19th century.

Southern Pacific's City of Industry–to–Oakland container train (symbol CIBAT) is led by locomotives from two rivals on July 6, 1994, as CSX B36-7 5860 and GP38-2 2639, along with Union Pacific SD40-2 3211, disturb the peace in the wildlife refuge in Alviso. Union Pacific would announce its intention to acquire Southern Pacific 13 months later.

The wildlife refuge was renamed on December 28, 1995, to honor Don Edwards (1915–2015), a longtime San Jose congressman, upon his retirement from public office. On November 20, 2015, Union Pacific train symbol OWWCJ is en route from South San Francisco to Utah led by GE ES44AC 5298 and AC4400CW 6077. The refuge is the largest wetlands restoration project in the United States outside of the Florida Everglades.

Two

Newark to Emeryville

The Capitol Corridor leaves the salt flats north of Alviso and arrives in Newark on trackage that once hosted the narrow-gauge horse-drawn railcars of the South Pacific Coast Railroad. In 1992, improved track and signals permitted Amtrak trains to make a right turn and continue towards the future station stops in Fremont and Hayward, which opened on June 4, 1993, and May 29, 1997, respectively.

The route continues through the suburban backyards of Hayward and San Leandro before entering the industrial detritus of East Oakland, where dense housing developments are being built upon land once home to a variety of heavy industries. Some builders have left the factories' tall water tanks intact amongst the new homes as a monument to the neighborhood's industrial past. A few industries survive, and even fewer see visits from Union Pacific freight trains to deliver and pick up freight cars.

The newest train station stop on the Capitol Corridor is Coliseum Station, which was dedicated on May 25, 2005, at the Oakland–Alameda County Coliseum complex. Consisting of just platforms and shelters, it is located between the stadium and the Bay Area Rapid Transit (BART) Coliseum Station, which opened on September 11, 1972.

After damage from the Loma Prieta earthquake forced Amtrak to vacant the Southern Pacific's 16th Street depot in West Oakland, a new depot was dedicated on May 12, 1995, at Alice Street and the Embarcadero in Oakland's Jack London Square, just south of downtown.

Like the stations between Oakland and San Jose, one-square-mile Emeryville was never an Amtrak stop but became one on August 13, 1993, when a new depot was opened on the site of a former asphalt plant. Amtrak passengers reach San Francisco by boarding Amtrak thruway buses here. The depot, now Amtrak's fifth-busiest in California, quickly became an anchor for postindustrial redevelopment in the area when a new hotel was built across the railroad tracks west of the station, followed by new condominiums and office buildings.

Upgraded track and signals installed in 1992 helped speed up Capitol Corridor trains between Newark and Fremont. On September 5, 1993, Amtrak Capitol train 723, led by EMD F40PH 290, turns from the Centerville Line toward the Mulford Line to San Jose. On the left is the Newark tower, which hosted an operator to control switches at this junction until 1985.

More right-of-way upgrades brought additional track and signals to this junction. On August 12, 2006, engineer Paul Jevert is at the controls of F59PHI 2005, which leads Amtrak Capitol train 741 towards San Jose at what Union Pacific calls Control Point (CP) Cherry. The Newark tower was removed in early 2003, technology having long rendered it obsolete.

The Denver & Rio Grande Western Railroad was much smaller than Southern Pacific when it acquired the latter in 1988, yet its small fleet of locomotives were frequent visitors to SP rails. On June 29, 1994, Rio Grande locomotives outnumber Southern Pacific's four to one on the West Colton–to–Warm Springs (Fremont) manifest (symbol WCWSM), which turns east onto the Centerville Line at Carter Street in Newark.

On March 20, 1993, Southern Pacific waged a "weed war" on it track through Newark when GP9E 3764 and 3843 led a herbicide-spraying train, complete with a caboose on the rear. Keeping the tracks clear of vegetation increases safety by eliminating visual obstructions and helps maintain proper drainage. In the distance is the steeple for St. Edward's Catholic Church, which was built in the 1870s.

An Amtrak test train, with engineer Phil Gosney in the cab of EMD F40PH 398, passes the Newark tower during a test trip on the newly rebuilt Centerville Line track from here to Fremont on July 3, 1992. This special move helped with the development of the schedule for the newest portion of the route, which would eventually include additional station stops in Fremont and Hayward.

A derailment on Union Pacific's former Western Pacific track through Fremont forced its trains to detour onto rival Southern Pacific's track through Newark in order to reach its freight yard in Oakland. On February 5, 1994, the St. Louis–to–Oakland expedited intermodal train (symbol SLOAZ) is in unfamiliar territory as it passes the Newark tower as it turns north on to the Mulford Line.

Engineer Phil Gosney and his one-car Amtrak Capitol test train pass the moribund Centerville depot on July 3, 1992. When the track through here first opened in 1881, the railroad did not have much of a fuel bill, since horses were used to haul train cars until Southern Pacific steam locomotives took over in 1909.

Southern Pacific opened its Centerville depot in 1910, and passenger trains stopped here until March 29, 1940. By 1961, the railroad closed the depot due to lack of business. For the next 30 years, various private companies occupied the building, the last being an electronics store that left in 1991. On March 27, 1993, the depot sits vacant awaiting its salvation as a passenger station once again.

Amtrak Capitol train service began stopping in Fremont at a makeshift platform across from the Centerville depot on June 4, 1993. Rather than build a new structure, the City of Fremont stepped in and acquired the depot that year. It was jacked up, turned around, and moved across the tracks and then underwent several years of restoration to return it to its 1910 appearance. Work is in progress as depicted on April 22, 1995.

Altamont Commuter Express ran a special train on October 16, 1999, to celebrate its one-year anniversary of scheduled train operations. The Capitol Corridor's second main track through this area needs an application of ballast rock before it can be used. This additional track will permit more passenger trains to be scheduled and help expedite Union Pacific freight trains past the restored depot. (Photograph by Jon Pullman Porter.)

On September 5, 1993, Southern Pacific's DOEUM, with mostly empty freight cars en route from Dolores yard in Long Beach to Eugene, Oregon, is hauled across Alameda Creek at Niles Junction by SD40T-2 8529, SD45R 7506, and SD40T-2 8301. Upon reaching the Beaver State, the train's freight cars will be reloaded with finished timber, and it will then return south to customers in California and elsewhere.

En route from its home in San Francisco to Oakland for weekend round-trips from there to Tracy for the latter city's annual Dry Bean Festival, former Southern Pacific Baldwin P8 4-6-2 Pacific 2472 crosses Alameda Creek in Fremont on July 29, 1993, with passenger cars painted in the brilliant and beautiful Daylight paint scheme introduced by Southern Pacific in the late 1930s.

The inaugural Capitol Corridor train is stopped under the Winton Avenue overpass in Hayward on December 11, 1991, while Amtrak's Arthur Lloyd speaks to the crowd from aboard business car *Beech Grove*. Rails reached Hayward in 1865, but the city had been without passenger service since 1941. A new Amtrak station at 22255 Meekland Avenue (near the overpass in the distance) would not open until May 29, 1997.

On March 5, 2012, F59PHI 2001 pushes Amtrak Capitol train 532 at the Coliseum Station, the newest station on the Capitol Corridor. It was dedicated on May 25, 2005, and serves the Oakland–Alameda County Coliseum complex. It is connected via a pedestrian platform to the nearby BART Coliseum Station. The Capitol Corridor has two different stations adjacent to stadiums used by professional football teams.

An 1/87 scale mode of Oakland's new Amtrak depot in Jack London Square (then under construction) was on display inside the California State Railroad Museum in Sacramento on June 18, 1994, during that year's Railfestival. The architects were from the VBN Architectural Firm in Oakland, while the general contractor was SHC Mark Diversified Construction Company. A highlight is the elevator-equipped pedestrian overpass, which was installed overnight on November 5–6, 1994.

The Airship Ventures dirigible *Eureka* N704LZ provided the elevation for this aerial view on November 13, 2011, of Amtrak's Oakland Jack London Square depot (with its double-vaulted roof) and the parking garage that opened on August 10, 2010. The rear two cars of Amtrak's 40th Anniversary Display Train are visible on the platform. After the depot was built, it attracted dense residential development to the neighborhood.

The new Amtrak depot's west side in Oakland's Jack London Square is seen on June 10, 1995. Dedicated on May 12, 1995, it is named for Cottrell Lawrence Dellums (1900–1989), a cofounder of the Brotherhood of Sleeping Car Porters. The new building brought Amtrak service back to the city after passenger trains quit serving the earthquake-damaged former Southern Pacific depot at Sixteenth and Wood Streets the previous year.

Wooden benches repatriated from inside the closed SP 16th Street passenger depot are seen inside the new Amtrak depot in Jack London Square on June 10, 1995. This view from inside the 5,000-square-foot atrium looks north towards Second Street with a sandwich shop's mural visible through the depot windows. Remarkably, this building is the 15th intercity passenger train depot constructed in Oakland but the first built for Amtrak.

Under a nearly full moon on the evening of June 11, 1995, Amtrak SSB1200 554, acquired from the Santa Fe Railway in 1984, drags the California Zephyr slowly from the new depot through the square past the towering Jack London Inn sign. Southern Pacific requested a locomotive on the rear of this particular train when it was moved to and from Amtrak's facilities in West Oakland Yard. The shift of Union Pacific's freight trains from the former Western Pacific main line on nearby Third Street, plus Amtrak's addition of mail and express cars on the back of its passenger trains, added to the congestion and delays here. This tedious move continued until October 26, 1997, when the Zephyr originated and terminated in Emeryville with a bus connection to Oakland.

Southern Pacific EMD SD70Ms 9815 and 9820 (both only a few weeks old) lead the Oakland–to–Long Beach intermodal container train (symbol OALBT) through Jack London Square on September 3, 1994. Although Southern Pacific bought only 25 of these innovative locomotives, its eventual owner Union Pacific ordered 1,000 of these 4,000-horsepower giants from the General Motors Locomotive Group in 2000.

The crowd takes a close-up look at the visiting Swedish Railways ABB X2000 train on display on the Southern Pacific track in Jack London Square on Embarcadero at Clay Street on July 10, 1993. The X2000 was modified so it could control a pushing diesel locomotive when it traversed trackage that was unplugged. The sleek electric trainset visited areas around the United States identified as potential high-speed rail corridors.

Engineer Phil Gosney climbs aboard Amtrak F40PH 395 just prior to departing the Southern Pacific 16th Street depot with San Joaquin train 702 for Bakersfield on April 10, 1994. Next to the train is the 16th Street interlocking tower, which has an operator inside to control track switches in and out of the area. Until its closure on October 12, 1995, this was the last active tower in the San Francisco Bay Area.

On June 15, 1994, former Southern Pacific Baldwin P8 4-6-2 Pacific steam locomotive 2472 leads a special train of Southern Pacific business cars en route to Sacramento at the closed Oakland depot. The building was constructed in 1912, only nine years before the steam locomotive, but was closed on October 17, 1989, due to damage from the Loma Prieta earthquake. Within several weeks, Amtrak trains would no longer stop here.

On July 17, 2015, Jim Maurer stood on the Adeline Street overpass in Oakland and captured this dramatic nighttime scene at the Amtrak locomotive and passenger car servicing facility in the former Southern Pacific West Oakland Yard. It was opened on October 12, 2004, and is the maintenance base for over 80 passenger cars and over 17 diesel locomotives. It is the newest Amtrak repair facility on the West Coast, along with Amtrak's large Redondo Junction complex

in downtown Los Angeles. In the distance are large cranes at the Port of Oakland as well as the San Francisco–Oakland Bay Bridge. Union Pacific's freight yard is on the left. This image serves as a reminder that rail transportation is a 24-hour-a-day, 365-day-a-year endeavor. (Photograph by Jim Maurer.)

One element of the reconstruction of the collapsed Interstate 880 was the reconstruction of the former Southern Pacific main line past the West Oakland Yard. This yard is now used primarily for intermodal container and trailer traffic as well as locomotive and freight car servicing, as seen on November 13, 2011. Some of the freight yard operations were moved to the former Southern Pacific yard in East Oakland, which was also rebuilt. The new main line cuts diagonally from bottom left to top right. The new Amtrak servicing facility is in the center, bordered by Interstate 880 on the right (now constructed at surface level) and Adeline Street on the left. The large white building in the upper center is Union Pacific's freight car repair shop, and the intermodal facilities are at the top of the photograph.

Southern Pacific's Warm Springs–to–Roseville freight train (symbol WSRVM), led by SD9E 4402 and SW1500 2687 (along with six other unseen locomotives), waits patiently as Amtrak San Joaquin No. 710, led by P32-8BWH 501, and Amtrak's California Zephyr, led by F40PHs 275 and 299, work the platforms at Emeryville depot on September 3, 1994. The depot had opened 13 months earlier, and track work was still in progress.

On May 10, 2014, one hundred thirty-five years to the day after the gold spike was driven at Promontory, Utah, engineer Phil Gosney guides Amtrak's National Train Day display train out of Emeryville back to Amtrak's service facility in West Oakland. The train is led by P42DC 12 and has one former New Jersey Transit Bombardier Comet coach and three Amtrak-California bi-level cars. The pedestrian overpass over the tracks was added in 1997.

Three

BERKELEY TO HERCULES

Berkeley's former Southern Pacific depot was built in 1913, and it has hosted various restaurants since the railroad gave up passenger train service in 1971. San Joaquin trains stopped here from January 22, 1986, through October 26, 1998. It has been a stop for Capitol Corridor trains since their inception.

Richmond became an Amtrak stop in January 1978, and four years later, a staffed depot with a ticket window and a small waiting area was opened on the east side of the tracks close to the BART station. On December 1, 1997, Amtrak closed the depot. The building remains in place but is unmarked and inaccessible. On October 18, 2006, the new Richmond Transit Center was dedicated. It features new Amtrak station platforms between the two main line tracks along with covered waiting areas accessible by either elevator or stairs. On the west side is a new transit bus terminal with a police substation. An adjacent five-story, 750-space parking garage for BART passengers was opened on May 30, 2013. Nearby is an interchange with Union Pacific short-line railroad partner Richmond Pacific Railroad. Chevron, the city's largest employer, has operated a large petroleum refinery here since 1902.

The route continues north through industrial North Richmond and then begins its scenic route along the south shoreline of San Pablo Bay through Point Pinole Regional Park. There are no Amtrak stops in this area, but the city of Hercules is building an intermodal transit center on the site of its namesake former explosives factory as part of this site's redevelopment. Another redevelopment project was the construction of a large housing development on the former Pacific Refinery site on the city's northeastern edge, adjacent to the Capitol Corridor tracks.

On December 11, 1991, the inaugural Capitol Corridor train stops at the former Southern Pacific depot, originally opened in 1913 and now a restaurant. Amtrak trains first stopped at Berkeley on January 22, 1986, when it was added to the route of the San Joaquin trains between Oakland and Bakersfield. However, San Joaquin trains ceased stopping here on October 26, 1998.

This colorful array of Capitol Corridor public timetables was issued from 1991 to 2001. Several of the covers feature images of future train equipment and its proposed paint schemes. During the first 10 years of Amtrak Capitol passenger train service, the number of daily round-trips increased from six to nine, and ridership increased from about 173,000 to 703,000.

The Richmond station platforms have seen much improvement since the inaugural Capitol Corridor train stopped here on December 11, 1991. Although Amtrak closed the depot building here on December 1, 1997, a new 800-foot center platform between the main-line tracks was dedicated four years later. The tall gentleman on the far right walking along the fence is renowned railroad photographer and author Richard Steinheimer (1929–2011).

On October 18, 2006, the new Richmond Transit Center was dedicated. It features new Amtrak station platforms between the two main-line tracks along with covered waiting areas accessible by either elevator or stairs, as seen in this April 10, 2008, photograph. On the west side is a new transit bus terminal. Richmond is the other Capitol Corridor stop where passengers can transfer directly to the BART system's trains.

The Golden Gate Railroad Museum's magnificently restored Southern Pacific Baldwin P8 4-6-2 Pacific 2472 is eastbound on its original owner's track near Richmond with a special excursion train to the Tracy Dry Bean Festival on the morning of August 1, 1993. This location was once known as Giant, the site of a namesake explosives company that operated here until 1960, and is now part of the Point Pinole Regional Shoreline Park.

The Amtrak-California F59PHI locomotives purchased in 1994 by the California Department of Transportation (Caltrans) for use on the Capitol Corridor Amtrak trains were put to work on the San Joaquin trains as well. On June 24, 1995, Amtrak San Joaquin No. 714 is led by F59PHI 2002 with four Horizon Fleet cars at Giant. Bi-level California cars will eventually replace these single-level Horizon cars on both the San Joaquin and the Capitol trains.

Southern Pacific's "Crockett Rocket," the moniker for one of the local freight trains that serves industries between its namesake city and North Richmond, scoots through Giant led by EMD SW1500 2593 with a short freight train on August 1, 1993. In the 1950s, Walt Disney reportedly bought the track from the narrow-gauge railroad that served the explosives factory here and used it to build Disneyland's railroad.

Southern Pacific's Kansas City, Missouri–to–Oakland intermodal container train (symbol KCOAF) is wrapping up its long trip from the Midwest as it rolls through the eucalyptus groves at Giant on June 24, 1995, led by SD70M 9824 and Cotton Belt GP60 9729. These trees were originally planted by the explosives factory to help shield the area from any accidental explosions.

On October 8, 1994, Amtrak EMD F40PHs 229 and 348, with Southern Pacific lounge *City of Angels*, chair coach 293, and the elegant railroad president's business car *Sunset*, are coupled ahead of the much shorter Talgo cars eastbound at Pinole while en route for display in Sacramento. Similar Talgo equipment was later acquired by the States of Washington and Oregon for regional Amtrak service there, but not in California.

Southern Pacific's eastbound West Colton–to–Klamath Falls, Oregon manifest freight train rolls through the bluffs in Pinole on March 2, 1996, led by EMD SD70M 9803, SD40T-2 8268, and SD70M 9824. This scenic area was added to Point Pinole Regional Shoreline the following year and is along the route of the San Francisco Bay Trail.

Streamlined EMD F units were once commonplace on the Southern Pacific and Amtrak but had been gone from Capitol Corridor rails for nearly 25 years until a special train operated by Royal Canadian Pacific Tours passed through Pinole on November 8, 2000, led by Canadian Pacific Railway FP7A 1400, F9B 1900, and GP38-2 3084. The passenger cars are restored relics from the 1920s and 1930s.

The name *Orient Express* usually refers to the elegant passenger train that runs in Europe. However, a company in the United States prefaced it with "American" and adopted the Orient Express paint scheme for its restored streamlined cars used in a new luxury North American train service that ran from 1989 to 2008. On August 26, 1995, Amtrak EMD F40PHs 405 and 329 lead the opulent train through Pinole.

Southern Pacific's westbound Portland, Oregon–to–Oakland freight train (symbol PTOAT) is led by SD40T-2s 8295 and 8546 along with Cotton Belt GP60 9660 at Pinole on October 4, 1992. In the 1870s, a large grain terminal was built on the shoreline to export wheat via ship, but little evidence of it remains today.

On October 13, 2002, ExpressTrak refrigerator car 74071 trails eastbound Amtrak San Joaquin train 716 at Pinole. Amtrak's venture into refrigerated express service only lasted from 2000 to 2006 but harkened back to the glory years of passenger railroading, where similar cars owned by the Railway Express Agency were hauled on premium passenger trains around the United States until finally replaced by trucks in the late 1960s.

Union Pacific's westbound Roseville–to–Mira Loma, California, quality manifest freight train (symbol QRVML), led by ES44AC 5262 and SD70M 4676, passes eastbound Amtrak Capitol train 738, pushed by EMD F59PHI 2011, in Hercules on April 30, 2006. The track and signal upgrades to the Capitol Corridor over the years have not only benefited passenger train service but have also helped improve freight train velocity on the route.

On August 22, 2010, a rolling museum of streamlined passenger cars (many of them "vista domes") comprises the consist of the Feather River Express, a special train run from Emeryville via the former Western Pacific Railroad's route through the scenic Feather River Canyon to Portola and back. Led by Amtrak GE P42DCs 201 and 189, the train is returning from a weekend visit during the annual Portola Railroad Days.

The famous Santa Fe Railway red-and-silver "warbonnet" paint scheme survives on the BNSF, albeit fading fast, literally. Ex–Santa Fe GE DASH 8-40CW 803 leads in faded glory as it joins with BNSF DASH 9-44CW 5231 and warbonnet-painted DASH 9-44CW 4703 to lead a westbound container train visiting Hercules on August 26, 2007. In 2008, Union Pacific persuaded federal regulators to oust most BNSF trains from the corridor.

On August 26, 2007, westbound Amtrak San Joaquin 713 receives a helping of horsepower in the form of ex–Santa Fe EMD SD40-2 6893 while Caltrans EMD F59PHI 2015 loafs on the rear. San Joaquin trains use the Capitol Corridor between Oakland and Martinez before shifting at Port Chicago to their namesake route on the former Santa Fe Railway (now BNSF) to Bakersfield.

Four

Rodeo to Martinez

Since 1896, Rodeo has been home to a petroleum refinery originally built by Union Oil and operated by Phillips 66 since 2001. Tracks pass through the refinery and through a 604-foot tunnel before emerging at an asphalt flatland that covers the former lead smelter site at Selby, a portion of which is used by Kinder-Morgan to unload ethanol from railroad tank cars.

It could be said this portion of the Capitol Corridor is a "bridge-to-bridge" route. In Crockett, the Carquinez Bridge's two spans carry Interstate 80 over its namesake strait, while the Benicia-Martinez Bridge's two spans carry Interstate 680 over the Suisun Bay. The Southern Pacific opened its Suisun Bay drawbridge between Martinez and Benicia in 1930, over 30 years before the first of two highway bridges was built there.

Crockett's preserved Southern Pacific depot is home to the Crockett Museum. Nearby is the massive California & Hawaii cane sugar mill, which opened in 1906. The mill is topped with a prominent, illuminated sign that features the company name and logo.

East of Crockett, rails journey through Carquinez Regional Shoreline, passing the rotting piers at Eckley and Port Costa. The latter was once the terminal for the largest railroad ferryboat in the world before the railroad bridge from Martinez to Benicia opened. Southern Pacific maintained a freight terminal here until 1959, when operations were shifted east to Ozol Yard in Martinez.

Martinez, named after Don Ignacio Martinez, a Mexican general who commanded the Presidio of San Francisco from 1822 to 1827, was also the boyhood home of major-league baseball hall-of-famer Joe DiMaggio. The city is also the reputed birthplace of the martini. Martinez is the junction with the former Southern Pacific Mococo Line, Amtrak's connection for its Oakland-Bakersfield San Joaquin trains via the BNSF Railway switch at Port Chicago. The Shell Oil refinery here opened in 1916. Southern Pacific 0-6-0 steam locomotive 1258, built in the railroad's Los Angeles General Shops in 1921, has been on display near the Amtrak depot since 1989.

Amtrak's westbound train 5, the California Zephyr, is seen at Lone Tree Point Regional Park in Rodeo on August 17, 2003, led by the General Electric trio of P42DCs 97 and 73 and P32-8BWH 500. The train has just passed through the metal jungle of pipes at the Phillips 66 petroleum refinery in the distance. The lead locomotive would eventually be repainted in the current Amtrak livery like the locomotive behind it.

Two express boxcars and two express refrigerator cars trail Amtrak's westbound train 5 in Rodeo on August 16, 2003. In 1997, Amtrak had entered the mail and express business with a flourish. But in September 2004, then-Amtrak president David Gunn announced, "Mail and express no longer makes business sense for Amtrak and has negatively impacted the quality of our passenger service so the decision has been made to exit the business."

It appears westbound Amtrak Capitol train 741, led by P42DC 134, and westbound Amtrak San Joaquin train 713, led by F59PHI 2006, are racing each other to their next stop in Richmond as they pass through Lone Tree Point Regional Park in Rodeo on June 27, 2009. Improved track and signals on the Capitol Corridor have enabled this operational flexibility to permit the operation of additional Capitol Corridor trains.

What could be called the sweetest portion of the Capitol Corridor is Crockett, the location of the California & Hawaii sugar refinery since 1906. On May 11, 2013, eastbound Amtrak Capitol train 732, pushed by F59PHI 2013, passes between the massive sugar mill and the former Southern Pacific depot on the right, now home to the Crockett Museum and an N-scale model railroad.

Below the Carquinez Scenic Drive bluffs, Union Pacific's westbound Roseville–to–Long Beach (Dolores Yard) freight train (symbol QRVDO), led by ES44ACs 5686 and 5770, passes the crumbling wooden Ozol Yard office, while eastbound Amtrak Capitol train 734, pushed by F59PHI 2006, approaches the Amtrak depot in Martinez on March 26, 2006. Union Pacific has assigned a whopping 9,000 horsepower to haul just nine freight cars.

On September 7, 2007, "President Bush" visited Ozol Yard in the form of Union Pacific SD70ACe 4141. Specially painted by the railroad in honor of the opening of the 41st president's library in Texas, the colors are more akin to presidential aircraft, not Union Pacific Railroad. The "presidential" locomotive was in town to haul a train of special safety equipment for display at the Dow Chemical plant in nearby Pittsburg.

Union Pacific local freight train YOA-55, the Benicia Flyer, led by GP38-2s 569 and 812, is seen from the east side of the Ozol Yard office on May 20, 2007. This former Southern Pacific building was moved here from West Oakland around 1962. On March 26, 2008, Union Pacific demolished the structure, having replaced it with a mundane white office trailer several months earlier.

Former Canadian National Railway FP9A 6304 (now privately owned) is appropriately clad in Southern Pacific paint as it leads a special train of privately owned passenger cars eastbound on the east side of Ozol Yard in Martinez on July 5, 2005. This train departed from Emeryville en route to Portland, Oregon, and would also take a side trip on short-line lumber hauler McCloud Railway in the Mount Shasta area.

The westbound Roseville–to–San Jose freight train (symbol MRVSJ), led by Southern Pacific SD40T-2 8271, Union Pacific SD60M 2179, and ex-SP GP38-2s 1516 and 1479, crosses over the Alhambra Creek bridge in Martinez on September 30, 2001. The new Amtrak depot on the right had only been open a few weeks.

In order to ensure the safety and integrity of the Capitol Corridor tracks, they are inspected frequently by Union Pacific employees. To look inside the rails where human eyes can't see, a specially designed track inspection car is used. On March 18, 2006, the EC-4's electronic equipment is hard at work as it slowly approaches the west side of the Amtrak depot in Martinez.

On September 24, 1994, Amtrak's westbound San Joaquin train 703, led by F40PH 380, unloads passengers at the Southern Pacific depot in Martinez. This building became woefully undersized once 20-plus Amtrak trains began stopping in town. Built in 1878, it is now a registered historic landmark, and the city hopes to convert it into a museum.

The new, larger Martinez depot was dedicated on September 22, 2001. It was built on the former site of a Southern Pacific maintenance complex west of the old depot. On September 29, 2001, Surfliner-painted F59PHI 461, visiting from Southern California, arrives with eastbound Capitol train 732. On the right, local transit and Amtrak thruway buses await their passengers.

Southern Pacific's Benicia Flyer local freight train passes the future site of the new Amtrak depot in Martinez on September 24, 1994. Led by unseen SW1500s 2671 and 2471, it is trailed by C-50-9 bay window caboose 4702, still earning its keep after most have been replaced by "end-of-train" (EOT) devices, a red-lighted electronic box about the size of a five-gallon fuel can on the rear freight car.

Single-level passenger cars returned on a regular basis to the Capitol Corridor when 14 former New Jersey Transit Comet 1B coaches were placed in San Joaquin train service in October 2013. On November 23, 2013, non-powered control unit 90218, a former Amtrak F40PH painted in the vintage 1985 peninsula Caltrain paint scheme, protects the rear of westbound Amtrak San Joaquin train 711 at the depot platforms in Martinez.

The eastbound California Zephyr Returns, a passenger special from Emeryville to the Western Pacific Historical Society Convention in Sparks, Nevada, stops at the Amtrak depot in Martinez on April 15, 2004. The train is led by Western Pacific–painted FP9A 906A and Amtrak P42DCs 168 and 142, along with Amtrak's ex–Great Northern full-length Budd vista dome car and five original California Zephyr passenger cars.

The Western Pacific Railroad, which was acquired by Union Pacific on December 22, 1982, operated the Oakland–to–Salt Lake City portion of the California Zephyr from 1949 to 1970. The Western Pacific never ran anywhere near Martinez, but these classic stainless steel streamlined passenger cars replicated what author and photographer Fred Matthews called "the zenith of the streamliner era."

Conductor Laurette Lee closes the baggage car door aboard eastbound Amtrak train 6, the California Zephyr, at the new depot in Martinez on February 9, 2003. Sadly, the Martinez native perished aboard her train on June 24, 2011, when a speeding tractor-trailer truck crashed through lowered crossing gates on US Route 95 and slammed into the Amtrak passenger car she was inside while westbound near Fallon, Nevada.

Eastbound Amtrak train 14, the Coast Starlight, led by P42DCs 120 and 112, pauses for its station stop in Martinez at 10:54 p.m. on June 1, 2002. The locomotives are in front of the former Southern Pacific depot. Since Amtrak moved out, the depot has been used by a costume rental store and as a temporary branch of the local public library.

Until the new repair shops opened in mid-2007 on the site of the former Southern Pacific Lenzen Avenue roundhouse in San Jose, Caltrain diesel locomotives sometimes hitched a ride on Capitol trains to and from the Union Pacific locomotive shops in Roseville. On January 6, 2007, MPI MP36PH-3 926 tags along with Amtrak-California EMD F59PHI 2011 eastbound on Capitol train 732 passing the former Southern Pacific depot in Martinez.

Union Pacific' westbound Benicia Flyer, led by Southern Pacific EMD GP40-2 7615, prepares for "landing" back in Ozol Yard as it crosses Ferry Street in front of the former SP depot in Martinez on September 29, 2001. Amtrak had moved to its new depot earlier in the month. The Southern Pacific depot (standard plan number one) was originally built with second-story living quarters, which were removed in 1942.

No one is aboard either locomotive—BNSF DASH 9-44CW 7700 and Helm Leasing (former Burlington Northern) SD40-2 7149—as they serve as distributed power units (DPU) for extra horsepower on the rear of BNSF Railway's westbound Chicago-to-Oakland (symbol S-CHIOIG) intermodal train passing the former SP depot in Martinez on May 19, 2007. A DPU is controlled by the engineer in the unseen lead locomotive.

Southern Pacific's Sacramento Shops built new steam locomotives from 1872 until 1937. In 2014, another company in Sacramento, Siemens Transportation Systems, began building new ACS-64 electric locomotives for use on Amtrak's electrified trackage between Washington, DC, and Boston. ACS-64s 639 and 638 begin their journey to the east coupled into Amtrak train 6, the California Zephyr, led by P42DCs 154 and 158 in Martinez on March 28, 2015.

Five

Benicia to Colfax

The Capitol Corridor makes landfall in Benicia after crossing the Suisun Bay drawbridge, the first of two movable bridges between Martinez and Sacramento. From February 3, 1853, to February 24, 1854, Benicia served as the state capital.

Leaving Benicia, tracks enter the Suisun Marsh, one of the largest remaining estuarine wetland areas in the continental United States. Dry land is reached at the next Amtrak stop in Suisun City.

Suburbia subsides yet again as the trackside landscape returns to agricultural use for several miles until Dixon, a city that missed its former Southern Pacific two-story combination depot so much it built an exact replica at its original location in 2006. Davis, meanwhile, has managed to keep and preserve its Mission Revival passenger depot, which opened in 1913. After returning to suburbia in West Sacramento, tracks cross the Sacramento River via the I Street swing bridge, which also hosts vehicular traffic on its upper level.

On the east side of the river 130 route miles from San Jose is Sacramento, California's state capital since 1854 and the western origin of Southern Pacific predecessor Central Pacific's transcontinental railroad. The Capitol Corridor's next Amtrak stop is in Roseville, amidst Union Pacific's massive J.R. Davis freight car classification yard and locomotive repair shop.

Leaving the Sacramento Valley, the tracks head east on a continuous upgrade on the route of the original transcontinental railroad. Rocklin, a city whose name may have originated from the numerous granite quarries which operated in the area until the last closed in 2004, is the next Amtrak Capitol Corridor stop. Here, in 1909, Southern Pacific opened the first portion of its second main track from the east on this mountainous railroad. When constructed, the additional track did not parallel the first. The route difference is quite evident in Auburn, where the Amtrak Capitol Corridor depot is on the east side of town while the other main line track passes through the city several blocks to the west. From January 26, 1998, through February 27, 2000, Amtrak Capitol Corridor train service continued east to Colfax, a stop for Amtrak's Chicago-to-Emeryville California Zephyr train since 1976.

The 5,603-foot-long Suisun Bay railroad drawbridge between Martinez and Benicia officially opened on November 10, 1930. It replaced Southern Pacific's huge railroad ferryboats, which had hauled trains across the bay waters between Port Costa and Benicia since 1879. On April 23, 1995, Southern Pacific's Richmond-to-Geneva Steel Works (Vineyard, Utah) petroleum coke train (symbol RIGVC) approaches landfall on the north end of the bridge in Benicia.

Union Pacific's westbound Roseville–to–San Jose freight train (symbol MRVSJ), led by Southern Pacific EMD SD40T-2 8250 and 8288, crosses the Sulfur Springs Valley Creek viaduct in Benicia as it climbs towards the Suisun Bay Bridge on April 9, 2000. Benicia is also a port for vehicle carriers and break-bulk cargo. A large Valero petroleum refinery (Exxon until 2000) is north of the tracks.

East of Benicia, the Capitol Corridor enters the Suisun Marsh, domicile of a wide variety of estuarine wildlife, including river otters, tule elk, and many different bird species. In September 1997, a Union Pacific train of automobile carriers led by AC4400CW 6733 with Norfolk Southern SD50s 6639 and 6623 heads westbound towards Oakland. *Suisun* is a Patwin Indian word meaning "west winds." (Photograph by Jamie Miller.)

Suisun City once had a railroad terminal that included an engine house. This downsized junction remains a freight car interchange between Union Pacific and short-line railroad partner California Northern Railroad, which operates the branch line from here to Napa and Vallejo. On November 25, 2012, Union Pacific's westbound Chicago-to-Milpitas, California, automobile carrier train (symbol AGBMI) has EMD SD70ACe 8666 as rear DPU as it passes Cordelia Road.

If a banner was not available for the inaugural Capitol Corridor train to break, a bottle of unknown spirits was. The rear coupler of Amtrak business car 10001, the *Beech Grove*, takes a beating from a bottle during the ceremonial train's stop at the Suisun-Fairfield depot on December 11, 1991. Amtrak's California Zephyr also stopped here until October 24, 1998. In 2015, the Capitol Corridor Amtrak trains that served this station were used by 163,769 passengers. This portion of Solano County has experienced rapid suburbanization since the 1990s, and as a result, local governments sponsored the construction of an additional Amtrak station in eastern Fairfield where Peabody Road crosses the tracks.

Southern Pacific renamed its Suisun City station Suisun-Fairfield in 1914 after the State Railroad Commission declared the railroad did not need two stations a mile apart from each other. A new colonnaded depot was constructed in 1913 a bit closer to Fairfield but still in Suisun City, and it was under restoration when the inaugural Capitol Corridor train made its ceremonial stop on December 11, 1991.

The colonnaded Southern Pacific depot in Suisun City was acquired by the city. As seen in this May 29, 1995, photograph, restoration was nearly complete. The other former colonnaded Southern Pacific depots that survive on the Capitol Corridor are the Niles depot in Fremont and the Colfax depot, but neither is a stop for Capitol Corridor passenger trains.

On May 6, 2006, the City of Dixon officially dedicated its new transportation center, whose centerpiece is an exact replica of the Southern Pacific depot built on the north side of the former Southern Pacific tracks utilized by Capitol Corridor trains. As part of the dedication festivities, a special Amtrak train ran from Emeryville to Dixon, pushed by F59PHI 2006. No passenger trains had stopped here since 1962.

The southeast side of the reconstructed depot is pictured on September 2, 2006. A pedestrian underpass below the tracks was opened in 2014 as part of the city's efforts to have Capitol Corridor passenger trains stop in Dixon. Additional fencing and trees now obscure this side of the depot, which currently houses the Dixon Chamber of Commerce. The original Dixon depot was built in 1884 but was razed in 1973.

Since this July 3, 1993, photograph, the empty landscape on the south side of the Davis depot has been turned into an attractive, landscaped pedestrian plaza. On October 10, 2008, the City of Davis dedicated this plaza in honor of A.G. "Sam" Brinley, who worked as a telegrapher and agent at this depot from 1913 until 1948. Built in 1913, the depot was extensively renovated in 1986.

On October 23, 1993, California Northern Railroad GP15-1 108, originally built in 1976 for the Chicago & North Western, brings freight cars past the depot in Davis to the interchange tracks. One month earlier, Southern Pacific had leased its 111-mile West Valley Line from Davis to Tehama to this new short-line railroad. Over 20 years later, Union Pacific continues this lease with its short-line partner.

Westbound Amtrak Capitol 725, led by F40PH-2 284, makes its station stop at Davis on June 15, 1994. During that year, Caltrans awarded $148,617 for improvements to the depot, including additional landscaping and the installation of 100 bicycle lockers. In 2016, the depot is a stop for 30 weekday Capitol Corridor trains, the daily Los Angeles–to–Seattle Coast Starlight, and the daily Emeryville-to-Chicago California Zephyr passenger trains.

The Davis depot platform has sprouted a forest of light poles as well as a bonanza of vegetation as westbound Amtrak Capitol 745 departs on May 6, 2006, led by P32-8BWH 2051. The same locomotive, then in its red, white, and blue paint scheme, led the inaugural eastbound Capitol Corridor train here on December 11, 1991.

It was already well over 85 degrees on the morning of July 3, 1993, when Amtrak EMD F40PH 247 stalled while leading eastbound Capitol train 722 shortly after departing the depot in Davis. Southern Pacific graciously offered to loan two diesel locomotives from a westbound sugar beet train (bound for the sugar mill in nearby Woodland) to haul the train for the remainder of its trip to Sacramento.

Between Davis and West Sacramento, the Capitol Corridor is carried by the Yolo Causeway, which is composed of levees and trestles. In winter, controlled releases of Sacramento River water fill the Yolo Basin, and the flooded area resembles an inland sea. On May 6, 2006, BNSF's lengthy Clovis, New Mexico–to–Oakland intermodal train (symbol S-CLOOIG) marches across the causeway in a strong showing of trackage rights.

Amtrak's inaugural Capitol Corridor train breaks a banner at the Southern Pacific depot in Sacramento late in the afternoon on December 11, 1991, after a triumphant tour of the new Amtrak intercity route from San Jose. During the previous 20 years, Amtrak only had four trains daily serving Sacramento, but in 2015, the station became the seventh-busiest on the entire Amtrak system, thanks primarily to the Capitol Corridor trains.

At 6:40 a.m. on June 20, 1998, the Mount Shasta Daylight, a chartered Amtrak train (sponsored by the Portola Railroad Museum) from Sacramento to Dunsmuir and back, awaits departure from the Sacramento depot led by F40PHs 397 and 390. Capitol train 733 is on the right. The eventual expansion of passenger train service on the Capitol Corridor resulted in the construction of additional station tracks.

On June 17, 1993, Southern Pacific's westbound Ozol Turn freight train slows for the curve just east of the Sacramento depot. In 2012, a major project rerouted the depot trackage through part of the former shop area in order to expand capacity and ease train congestion. The track relocation project eliminated this curve in favor of a straighter route to the north for Union Pacific's freight trains.

Sacramento Regional Transit light-rail vehicles CAF 208, Siemens 117 and 115, and CAF 211, arrive at the Sacramento depot from H Street on April 10, 2008. Light-rail service to what is now called the Sacramento Valley Station began on December 8, 2006. On the left are the Capitol Corridor main tracks, which were removed and relocated 1,000 feet to the north in 2012.

Amtrak San Joaquin train 708, with P42DC 157, prepares to depart the Sacramento depot (seen on the far right) on September 11, 2008. On February 21, 1999, Amtrak's San Joaquin trains began serving Sacramento when service was extended north on the former Southern Pacific from the junction with BNSF in Stockton. The Robert T. Matsui United States Courthouse, opened in 1999, towers above the scene.

The original passenger platform tracks were removed in 2012 as part of the depot's expansion project as well as to clear the area for the proposed redevelopment of the former Southern Pacific shops. The aftermath appears on November 24, 2012. The light-rail tracks on the far right remain in use.

On August 13, 2012, the platforms at the relocated depot trackage were placed in service. This view, taken on November 24, 2012, from the old platforms closer to the depot, shows the vacant land targeted for development while westbound Amtrak Capitol trains 741 (led by F59PHI 2008) and 743 (led by F59PHI 2010) await departure adjacent to the former Southern Pacific shop complex, which operated from 1868 until 1992.

What the station's redevelopers called the "path to progress" is illustrated by the new tunnel network under the Sacramento depot tracks that passengers must navigate to reach their trains. On November 24, 2012, the video monitor with the train platform assignments does the job formerly the domain of interchangeable signs.

The Southern Pacific name is still proudly displayed on the Sacramento passenger depot on November 24, 2012. The City of Sacramento purchased the depot, opened in 1926, from Union Pacific in 2006, and it is undergoing a complete renovation. On March 19, 2016, the depot's new Amtrak ticket counter was opened in the west side of the building's ground floor.

The crowd listens to speeches inside the Southern Pacific depot in Sacramento on December 11, 1991, after the arrival of the inaugural Amtrak Capitol Corridor train from San Jose. The depot was opened in 1926, and a mural above the scene by John MacQuarrie (who also painted the mural inside the San Jose depot) illustrates California governor Leland Stanford breaking ground for the transcontinental railroad in Sacramento in 1865.

Sacramento's Elvas interlocking tower, built in 1911, controlled Southern Pacific's junction between its tracks from the Bay Area and its tracks going north and south. On July 19, 1997, Union Pacific's westbound Kansas City, Missouri–to–Oakland automobile carrier train (symbol AKSOA) passes the tower, led by a Wisconsin Central SD45 6632 along with Union Pacific SD9043MAC 8150. The tower was closed on November 1, 1999. (Photograph by Gary Perazzo.)

Pictured is the rebuilt former Southern Pacific yard in Roseville, including additional trackage that directs Capitol Corridor passenger trains around the busy yard operations. On June 11, 2005, eastbound Amtrak Capitol train 738, pushed by F59PHI 2002, passes Control Point West Atkinson on the edge of J.R. Davis Yard, renamed after its rebuilding in 1999 in honor of the last president of the Southern Pacific.

A herd of Southern Pacific diesel locomotives awaits its turn on the east side of the locomotive shop in Roseville on July 5, 1996. Union Pacific continues to operate the facility, which has been upgraded to service 21st-century low-emission diesel locomotives. This shop is also home to many of the railroad's fleet of former Southern Pacific rotary snowplows, spreaders, and flangers (the latter remove snow between the rails).

On June 8, 1997, eight months after the Union Pacific takeover, there are still Southern Pacific locomotives working in Roseville yard. On the left, GP60 9776 leads the eastbound Oakland–to–Kansas City automobile train (symbol AOAKS). In the middle is the eastbound Oakland-to-Eugene freight train (symbol MOAEU) led by SD45T-2 9329. On the right, AC4400CWs 372 and 211 lead the eastbound empty unit coal train (symbol CTASK).

Southern Pacific's eastbound Los Angeles–to–Portland, Oregon expedited intermodal train (symbol LAPCX), led by GP60 9733, SD45Rs 7530 and 7518, and SD45T-2 9381, appears to be getting a bath from the switchman assigned to the 245 (track switch) herder job on July 6, 1996. In reality, he is just watering down the gravel road to reduce dust.

Purchased while steam locomotives still plied the Southern Pacific, SD7Rs 1518 and 1519 were both rebuilt in early 1980 and were still valued members of the railroad while they switched freight cars near the depot in Roseville on March 12, 1995. The 1518 was the first of its model ever produced by the Electro-Motive Division of General Motors and now has a place of honor at the Illinois Railway Museum.

On July 5, 1996, westbound Amtrak Capitol train 723, with F59PHI 2007, awaits departure from the depot in Roseville. The depot was dedicated on March 4, 1994, and is modeled after the Southern Pacific standard plan two-story depot number 22. The previous depot, a colonnaded structure built in 1907, was razed in 1972.

The rear of the Roseville depot is seen on July 6, 1996. A travel agency currently uses the building, and there is a waiting room for Amtrak and Greyhound bus passengers. Only Amtrak Capitol Corridor passenger trains currently stop at the depot. The city rose to prominence when Southern Pacific relocated its rail terminal from Rocklin to Roseville in 1908.

Southern Pacific's westbound Utah–to–Long Beach export coal train, led by AC4400CWs 284 and 201 along with SD40T-2 8544 and SD40-2M 8578, emerges from 991-foot tunnel 18 in Newcastle on July 6, 1996. Opened in 1912, this is the only double-tracked tunnel between Rocklin and Colfax and was built as part of the project to add a second main track over the Donner Pass.

Union Pacific's eastbound Oakland–to–Kansas City, Missouri, auto carrier train (symbol AOAKS) climbs upgrade on number two track in Rocklin on June 8, 1997. The train is led by Southern Pacific GP60 9772, SD40T-2 8258, Union Pacific SD40-2 B4226, and a Southern Pacific SD45R. Capitol Corridor trains began stopping in Rocklin, Auburn, and Colfax on January 26, 1998.

Southern Pacific's eastbound Roseville–to–Kansas City, Missouri, freight train (symbol RVKCM), led by SD40T-2Ms 8624, 8585, and 8619 and SD45T-2 9373, crosses the massive viaduct over Interstate 80 in Auburn on July 6, 1996. The 540-foot structure was built in 1911–1912 as part of Southern Pacific's construction of an additional main track over the Donner Pass, anointed by author and photographer Richard Steinheimer (1929–2011) as "the mountain soul of the Southern

Pacific." Because of the two different main-line tracks through town, separate stations were in use for each Capitol Corridor passenger train direction until October 1998. Auburn opened a new passenger station and transit center at 277 Nevada Street on December 18, 2003. On March 14, 2008, a ceremony was held to rename the center in honor of the late Robert F. Conheim (1943–2007), a Placer County transit advocate.

To assist heavy eastbound trains over the Donner Pass, extra locomotives were often added here at Colfax. On July 7, 1996, a brakeman has just lined the track switch so Southern Pacific SD40T-2 8500 and SD45T-2R 6842 can get ready to be placed in a freight train. This procedure was conducted here rather than in Roseville to avoid delaying trains there. Colfax's colonnaded passenger depot was restored in 2007.

Rotary snowplows are the weapon of choice to remove heavy snowfall from the railroad over the Donner Pass. Each has a large rotating blade that picks up the snow and throws it far to the side. On March 25, 1995, Southern Pacific rotary snowplows MW 207 and MW 211 are spliced by their power units and locomotives in Colfax. Rotary snowplows were first deployed here in 1888. (Photograph by John Black.)

Bibliography

Bender, Henry E. Jr. *Southern Pacific Lines Standard-Design Depots.* Wilton, CA: Signature Press, 2013.

Demoro, Harre W. and John N. Harder. *Light-rail Transit on the West Coast.* New York: Quadrant Press, 1989.

MacGregor, Bruce A. and Richard Truesdale. *South Pacific Coast: A Centennial.* Boulder: Pruett Publishing, 1982.

Matthews, Fred. *Northern California Railroads–The Silver Age, Vol. 2.* Denver: Sundance Publications, 1984.

Neves, Victor and Brian Jennison. *Southern Pacific Sacramento Division.* Bucklin, MO: White River Publications, 2006.

Signor, John R. *Donner Pass: Southern Pacific's Mountain Crossing.* San Marino, CA: Golden West Books, 1985.

———. *Southern Pacific's Western Division.* Wilton, CA: Signature Press, 2003.

Steinheimer, Richard and Dick Dorn. *Diesels Over Donner: Mountain Soul of the Southern Pacific.* Glendale, CA: Interurban Press, 1989.

Tatam, Robert Daras. *Old Times in Contra Costa.* Pittsburg, CA: Highland Publishers, 1996.

Warner, David C. and Elbert Simon. *Amtrak by the Numbers.* Bucklin, MO: White River Publications, 2011.